Go along with Willie on all of his adventures!

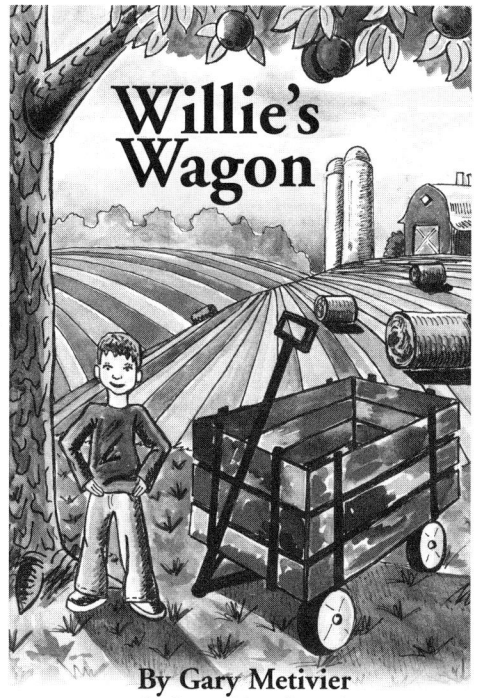

Visit
www.willieswagon.com
for more information

What Willie readers are saying about his first adventure

"It's the best children's book I ever read!!! It's really nice!!!"
-Grace R., second grader

"It's an amazing book! Also, it's my sister's favorite book." *-Paola V., fourth grader*

"I read the book every night. Thank you! My mom and I read it a lot. Keep on writing!"
-Makala

"I hope I can make a difference in someone's life."
-William B.

"Willie is cool!"
-Payton, second grader

"I love to help others. I cannot wait until your next book comes out."
-Anna

"I loved your book! I am just a thirteen-year-old girl and my words don't mean much, but you write awesome books!"
-Chelsea S.

"I liked it from the beginning to the end. At the end it was a little sad…and happy too."
-Lauren A., seven years old

Parents and teachers love Willie too!
(but we won't note their ages)

"This story not only teaches the lesson of giving but also teaches students to be thankful. This heartwarming story is touching to all ages of students and adults."
-Michelle R., teacher/LMC director

"Congratulations on writing a wonderful story!!! I read it to my seven-year-old daughter and my two-year-old son. My daughter wants to get all the Willie books she can!"
-Lisa M.

"Your message is wonderful for all ages."
-Tabatha C.

"My 12-year-old read it the second we got home and then told us, 'What a great story! That guy is going to go far!!' I just loved that!"
-Darcie M.

"Our son Logan is only four months old, but I read to him every night and I think Willie's Wagon needs to be a part of his library. I am extremely excited about the overall message and hope that someday Logan will be able to point to your book and say, 'I learned something from that book!'"

-Mike B.

"This book is my favorite! It reminds me of Alex's lemonade stand. Way to go!"

-Morgan P.

"This story inspired my students to think of ways they can make a difference to someone in their lives. It teaches them that their actions can have a positive effect on the lives of others and themselves."

-Keta F., teacher

A Willie's Wagon® Adventure

A hog ate my homework!

To My Buddy Josh!!

Your Friend 2008

A Willie's Wagon® Adventure

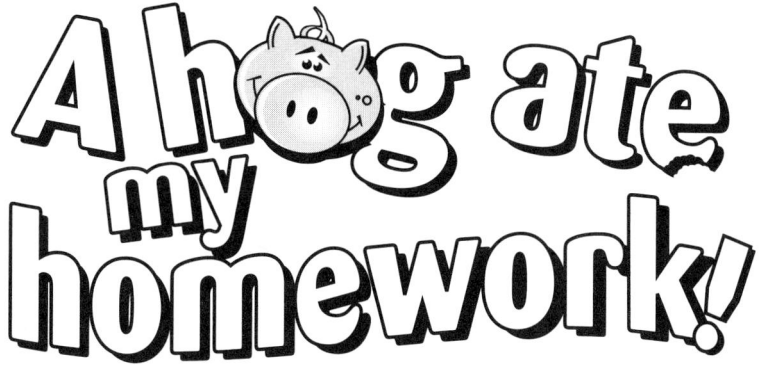

A hog ate my homework!

By Gary Metivier
Illustrated by David Houk

This book is dedicated to all who teach
our children–in and out of the classroom.

A Hog Ate My Homework!
A Willie's Wagon® Adventure

Written by Gary Metivier
Illustrations by David Houk
Book design by Becky Heidgerken

Printed in the USA.

Table of Contents

Chapter 1

The First Report

The morning school bell rang. Mrs. Specklefish held up two fingers–her usual sign that the second graders should stop talking and pay attention.

"I know most of you worked very hard on your first reports," she said, holding a stack of papers. "I have carefully looked over each one."

Willie got nervous. He knew he didn't do his best on his report. He swung his feet so much they bumped into the back of Lauren's chair.

"Willie! Stop hitting my chair," she whispered, hoping the teacher wouldn't hear.

Willie had already gotten her into trouble a few times in class. You see, Willie had the record for

1

getting red cards. The first time you're caught talking or not paying attention, you get a yellow card. The second time you get an orange card. The orange card means "watch out." The third time you get the dreaded red card. Red cards have to be taken home and signed by your mom or dad. That way they know you got in trouble at school. Willie thought anything after the red card would mean prison time, or even worse, no recess for a week!

Willie wasn't a bad student. In fact, he was very smart for his age. But sometimes he just got bored. That was the case when he received his first real writing assignment.

Mrs. Specklefish slowly moved from desk to desk, handing out the graded reports one by one. The report was supposed to be about what the students wanted to do when they grow up.

"Nice work, Jenna. I really enjoyed your story. It's

nice that you want to help sick children. 'Doctor Jenna' sounds good to me."

She headed down Willie's row. "Great job, Ryan. I see you are reaching for the stars. Make sure you pay extra attention in math and science. You'll need that to be an astronaut."

Mrs. Specklefish was now just three desks away from Willie. She came to his paper in the stack and stopped. Teacher looked at it closely, squinted her eyes, and carefully looked at Willie. *This is pure torture!*

Willie wanted to jump out of his seat and make a run for it. He was sure she would hate what he'd written. Mrs. Specklefish moved closer and set the paper on the edge of his desk. She spoke calmly and softly.

"Willie, I'm not sure you understood the assignment."

Willie's paper didn't have much writing on it. Most of the other papers were a full page long. Willie had less than half a page and there was plenty of space left.

"I put some notes on the back," she said. "I would like you to look over those notes with your parents and have them sign it. Willie, you're a good student. I think you can do better. I'd like you to try again."

His teacher finally moved on to the next desk. Willie could breathe now. His teacher was done with him, but his parents would have to see how awful his report really was. Willie felt doomed. His only hope was that his parents wouldn't ask about his day at school. But they *always* asked about his day. Now it was just a matter of time. Willie wasn't bored any more. He was *doomed!*

5

Chapter 2

Chicken and Butterflies for Dinner

Willie's favorite dinner sat in front of him: chicken, mashed potatoes, and peas. But Willie wasn't hungry. He felt like his belly was already full of butterflies. As he pushed his peas into the mountain of mashed potatoes, he thought this could be his last meal. After all, he knew what would come next.

"How was school today?" Dad asked.

Yikes! Willie bit down on his lip. He

7

squeezed the spoonful of mashed potatoes so hard that his fingertips turned red.

"Willie failed his first report!" his older sister Ashley blurted out. "Annie's sister told me all about it." For a moment Willie felt tempted to toss his spoonful of potatoes in the direction of his sister. She was better in school. She always did things right. And now she had to announce his *failing* to the entire world! Life as he knew it was over.

Ashley was a nice girl, but there was something about her little brother that just brought out the worst in her. Maybe it was how he always grossed out her fifth-grade friends when they came over. Maybe it was because he always left her stuck with his chores. Or just maybe it was because that's the way brothers and sisters sometimes treat each other growing up.

But right now Willie wasn't thinking about growing up. He just hoped to make it through dinner!

"Willie, I didn't even know you had an assignment due," Mom said. "I wanted to work with you on that. Let's see what you wrote."

Willie didn't say a word. He got up and shuffled toward his backpack on the floor near the front door. He looked at the backpack. Then he looked at the door. Willie thought, *If I make a run for it, maybe they'll never see the paper!*

He'd heard of kids running away. He could join the circus, but the circus wasn't in town. He could be a hobo on the train, but he didn't know what a hobo was.

Willie decided it was better just to give up, hand over his paper, and hope for the best. He imagined

9

handcuffs, striped jail pajamas, and bars holding him in his least favorite place in the house–his sister's girlie, pop-star decorated, pink room!

"Read it to us, Willie," Dad said as he crossed his arms and leaned back in his chair.

Great! Willie thought. *Not only do they want to see my failed report, they want me to* read *it too!*

Willie swallowed hard and read.

I would like to be a farmer when I grow up, because farming is easy!

They don't need to go to school, because they just play in the dirt and ride around on ATVs. When it rains, you can just stay inside and watch TV and play video games. When the sun comes back out, the corn just grows

out of the ground by itself. In the fall, someone comes by, cuts it down, and gives the farmer a bunch of money. They use that money to buy candy and more video games. The end.

When Willie dared enough to look up, he saw that the smiles on his parents' faces were gone. But instead of being mad, his mom looked disappointed.

She got up from the table and headed to the telephone. Was she calling the army to have him sent away to boot camp? She could be calling the television people to have his favorite shows turned off. Or, worst of all, would she dare put his video games up for sale on the Internet?

She pushed the buttons on the telephone one by one. With each button pressed, Willie sunk down lower and lower into his chair. *I'm doomed! I am only eight years old and my life is over!*

Chapter 3

Mom, the Judge

What would Willie's sentence be for doing a bad job on his school paper? Mom was the judge and the jury. She hung up the telephone and turned to Willie with the verdict.

"Looks like you are going to see firsthand what farmers do. My Uncle Kenny and Aunt Sandy have invited you to their family farm," she said. "We'll take you there this weekend. It's harvest time, and they are very busy, but they want you to see what a working farm is *really* like."

"Whatever." Willie moaned and rolled his eyes. He didn't want to go to the farm. But he also didn't want to get in any more trouble with his mom and dad.

15

"Can I go too?" Ashley asked with an excited voice. "Maybe they'll let me bottle-feed a baby animal or play with a goat!"

Willie gave her a look. "What are you going to do–paint the pigs' fingernails pink and dress them up like princesses?"

"Maybe I will," she answered as she crossed her arms and shook her head with attitude. "At least *I'm* not the one in trouble."

Willie didn't pay attention to her anymore. Instead, he crammed his favorite things into his backpack for the trip. As he tossed the backpack into the backseat of the pickup truck, he saw something in the garage he hadn't thought about in a long time–his wagon.

Willie found an old worn-out wagon on a trip to an apple orchard last year. Fixing up the wagon cured his boredom for a while. He spent a whole

week after school making it look as good as new. He used leftover paint from the garage–so this wagon had all sorts of colors on it.

The wagon inspired him to make a difference by helping sick children. He heard that some kids would have to miss the big field trip to the pumpkin patch, because they had to stay in the hospital until they got better. So Willie filled his wagon full of pumpkins and brought the pumpkin patch to them. He remembered how good that made him feel.

He grabbed an old rag and wiped some spider webs off the wagon handle and smiled at his old friend. *I wonder if this old wagon can help me get out of this mess,* Willie thought. *It's worth a try.* He loaded the wagon into the back of the truck as a neighbor watched. She looked kind of like Willie's grandma with puffy bluish-gray hair and a nice smile. She waved at him. Maybe it was a *hello* wave. Or maybe it was a *see-ya-wouldn't-want-to-be-ya* wave. He gave a quick wave back and got into the truck.

Chapter 4

Headed to
the Pen

The family pickup bounced around on the gravel road heading to the farm. Willie and Ashley had fun flopping around every time Dad hit a big bump. Good thing they had their seatbelts on or they would be in Mom's lap in the front seat!

While they enjoyed the bumpy ride, Dad mumbled something about the little rocks hitting his new truck. Willie looked out the back window to make sure the wagon didn't fall out. All he could see was the wagon and a cloud of dust behind them.

Uncle Kenny and Aunt Sandy met them on the big front porch. While most people have just a little porch on the front of their house, this house had one that went all the way around!

"You got here just in time. Looks like the rain is over for now," Aunt Sandy said as she gazed at the sky.

Uncle Kenny noticed the wagon in the back of the truck. "I haven't seen a wagon like this in years. And I've *never* seen one so colorful! Let's get it unloaded and put it in the barn."

Once inside the farmhouse, Uncle Kenny pulled off his work boots. "You have to try some of Auntie's homemade peach pie. It's the best in the county!"

Aunt Sandy frowned a little. "Oh, come now. This is a no-bragging zone." Her smile reappeared as she winked at Ashley, then they sat down in the living room.

Willie's parents ate the pie while they talked . . .
and talked . . . and talked. Willie and Ashley
wondered if they'd ever stop talking. They thought
this was sooooo boring! They looked around in the
old farmhouse. There were quilts on the couches
and chairs, and even quilts on the walls! Little

figurines lined the tops of every shelf. In the corner there was a collection of miniature green farm tractors. *That's strange*, Willie thought. *There aren't any kids who live here to play with them.*

Something was missing from this room. Willie's eyes opened wide when he figured out what it was. There were no video game systems attached to the big old TV! *How do these people live without video games?* Willie thought. *Even more important, how am I going to live for a whole weekend without them? I knew this was going to be punishment, but this—this is torture!*

His parents were about to leave. And now Willie, with only his sister to turn to, was officially stuck!

Chapter 5

Curly, the Cow

"Ashley, I hear you would like to feed a calf," Aunt Sandy said.

"I sure would!" she answered happily.

Aunt Sandy handed her a super-sized baby bottle, and they all walked to the barn. Willie followed them.

"We are helping our grandson raise a calf as part of his 4H project. Curly is just two weeks old." She patted the calf. "Willie, you can hold the rope while your sister feeds her. Hold on tight–Curly is hungry!"

Willie tried to pull the calf out of the barn to eat. At first, Curly wouldn't budge. But when she saw

the bottle of milk, she moved so quickly she dragged Willie behind her.

Ashley held on as Curly gulped down her meal. But when the calf drooled and spit the leftovers in her direction, she shouted, "Okay, I think I'm done with this chore!"

Willie laughed at his sister. Uncle Kenny put his hand on the boy's shoulder. "I have some chores for you too, young man. The pigs are hungry. How about giving me a hand?"

"Okay, I guess so." Willie shrugged.

"You'd better take off those new white tennis shoes. Here, put these old boots and coveralls on." Kenny handed him some old clothes.

"Whatever." Willie sighed as he tossed his shoes aside. "Maybe I could just go barefoot."

27

Uncle Kenny smiled and said, "I guess you haven't been around hogs before. Get dressed and we'll learn a little about my porker pals. And don't forget your notebook. You should get some good notes for your school paper."

Chapter 6

The Hog Hotel

Uncle Kenny and Willie were all dressed and ready to go. It was time to feed the pigs.

They walked toward a huge metal building where the hogs lived. In front of the building was a large area with a white fence around it.

"Willie, hogs don't sweat. When I was a boy, after a rain like we just had, the hogs would cool off in the mud puddles out there. Today they keep cool inside this building with the help of fans and water sprinklers," Uncle Kenny explained.

The farmer opened the big sliding door just enough to let the boy peek inside.

"Which ones are pigs and which ones are hogs?"

Willie asked.

"The little ones are pigs. The big ones are older. We call them hogs."

Willie looked at the bucket of apples the farmer had in his hand. "What do they eat?"

"They would eat just about *anything* you tossed in front of them," the farmer said with a laugh. "When I was your age, I used to 'slop' the pigs."

"Slop the pigs—what's that?" the boy asked, crinkling his nose at the word *slop*.

"We took the leftover skim milk from our cows, mixed it with some oats in a big barrel, and poured it into a trough." He brushed a fly off his nose. "In the summer, the slop attracted as many flies as it did hogs."

"These pigs eat a healthy and balanced meal out of feeders and stay in this barn."

"Do you want to give them a treat?" Willie

nodded. "The apples in this bucket are from our apple trees. Toss a couple in."

"Can't I just let them eat out of my hand?"

"Oh no." Kenny shook his head. "I'm afraid they might take a little more than just the apple."

"Can I go inside and feed them?" Willie asked.

"I feed them in a special place out back. From here, it's best if you just throw the apples in. While you do that, I'm going to check the feed in the grain bins." Uncle Kenny set the bucket down and walked off.

Willie looked around. It was just him and the pigs and hogs. They looked harmless enough. *Why can't I go in and pet one?* Willie thought. *Then I can write in my report what they feel like. I may never see another pig up close again. This is my chance.*

Willie looked around again—nobody in sight. No

31

one would ever know. He decided to make his own adventure. *I'm going for it*, he thought. *I'm going in.*

With his notebook in one hand and the bucket of apples in the other, Willie opened the barn door wider. He was about to learn a lesson he would never get at school. It would also be a lesson he'd never forget.

Chapter 7

Who Let The Hogs Out?

"Here piggy-piggies," Willie called out as he walked into the barn–a place he knew he really wasn't supposed to be. The pigs didn't seem to mind. They paid no attention to him.

Willie reached into the bucket and took out one apple. He dropped it just in front of his feet. A big hog waddled over, opened its mouth, and bit down on the end of Willie's work boot.

"Owwww. Stop that!" Willie yelped as he dropped the bucket of apples. The bite on the boot didn't really hurt, but he didn't want his foot to become a chew toy.

The noise got the attention of the other hogs. They discovered the spilt bucket of apples. All of a sudden, one pig ran for Willie. Then another. Then all of them were on the move like a buffalo stampede!

Willie stepped backward. He grabbed for the door and tried to pull it closed, but it was too late. The giant bacon bits came full speed ahead. It was like they were in a race—and Willie happened to be right in their path.

All of them tried to squeeze through the barn door at the same time.

Willie panicked. He turned and tried to run out of the way but tripped over a hog that somehow got behind him.

Willie splashed into a mud puddle in what used to be the pigpen just outside the barn. His notebook flew into the air.

The hogs surrounded Willie. Some of the hogs rolled in the mud puddles and made a big mess.

Willie curled up in a ball and covered his head with his arms, like in a school tornado drill.

Suddenly, he heard a barking sound. He peeked through his arms. In a flash, a dog leapt through the fence and ran right for Willie. The dog chased the pigs away. It barked loudly and nipped at the pigs' heels.

Willie felt a big tug on the back of his overalls. Uncle Kenny pulled him up and lifted him over the fence.

"Willie, I told you it was best to stay out of there. Hogs can be dangerous."

The dog crawled back through the fence and licked Willie's face. "Good thing Ol' Jack here came to the rescue," the farmer said.

"He really showed those hogs who's boss," Willie

said as he pet the dog.

"Ol' Jack is the best hired hand I ever had. We picked him up from the humane society a few years back. He's part border collie, so he has a talent for being around farm animals. He makes sure the pigs don't sneak up behind me, so I don't end up like you just did."

"Hey!" Willie shouted, pointing to the pigs. "That hog just ate my homework!" He watched the last bits of his notebook disappear.

"It seems the hogs like what you've written so far," the farmer said with a laugh.

Willie's nose twitched. He noticed a smell coming from the mud in his hair. The mud covered most of his body. "Why is this mud so . . . stinky?"

"Oh, that's not just mud, Willie!" the farmer explained, trying to hold back a big belly laugh. "Let's just say the hogs were doing more than

playing in the mud. I think it's time we get you cleaned up. I have to get these guys back inside and clean up this mess."

Even with more chores to do, Uncle Kenny still had a big smile on his face.

Chapter 8

Peach Pie

Willie soaked in the bath and washed off the pig smell. He could hear his sister Ashley talking with Aunt Sandy in the kitchen one room over.

"Is your peach pie really the best in the entire county?" Ashley asked, remembering what Uncle Kenny had said earlier.

"Well, it did win the top prize in last year's county fair," Aunt Sandy said with a smile. "But I don't want to brag about it. Maybe I just got lucky."

"How did you learn to make pie? Did you follow the directions on the side of the pie box?"

"No such thing as a pie box." Aunt Sandy placed

41

a bowl of fresh eggs on the counter. "I make it from scratch."

"What's *scratch*?" Ashley asked.

"That's when you make everything yourself." Aunt Sandy cracked an egg on the side of the bowl. "I mix up all the fresh ingredients myself. I use a recipe handed down from my mother and my grandmother. The peaches are from our own peach trees."

Ashley grabbed a fresh peach and tossed it from one hand to the other. "Do all girls on farms know how to cook like that?"

"No, not everyone. There was a time when that was our main job on the family farm. We did all the cooking, cleaning, and mending. Years back we even washed our own clothes by hand. Keeping up with everything was a full-time job. Nowadays we have things like washing machines and microwaves that

help. That gives us time to do other things."

"You didn't have a microwave back then?" Ashley exclaimed, wide-eyed with surprise. "How did you cook food?"

"We cooked in the oven or on the stove!" Aunt Sandy answered as she reached for a large wooden spoon. "Now I have a full-time job that has nothing to do with farming. I work for the post office delivering mail. A lot of farmers these days have jobs off the farm too."

"So why do you still bake your own pie if you can just get it at the store?" Ashley asked.

"Homemade tastes soooo much better. And it's fresher too." She grabbed a bowl and attached it to her electric mixer. "Plus, I want to keep the traditions alive. That's why I still bake. That is also why I make quilts and can lots of fresh fruit and vegetables from our trees and garden."

Now Ashley was very interested. "I get to help you make a pie with these peaches?"

"Sure! Let's get to work!" She pointed to a big canister on the counter. "You grab the flour and I'll get my secret family ingredient."

"Wow, you have a secret! You have to tell me!" Ashley begged.

Sandy reached into the refrigerator. "Since it's a secret, I have to whisper it. But you have to keep it between us girls."

Willie was still in the bath, listening to their conversation. He leaned out of the tub and tried to hear the secret. But they whispered so quietly he couldn't hear. Willie stretched and stretched even farther. He looked like a turtle with its head stuck out of its shell as far as it would go.

I have to know the secret, he thought. He was now barely in the tub.

45

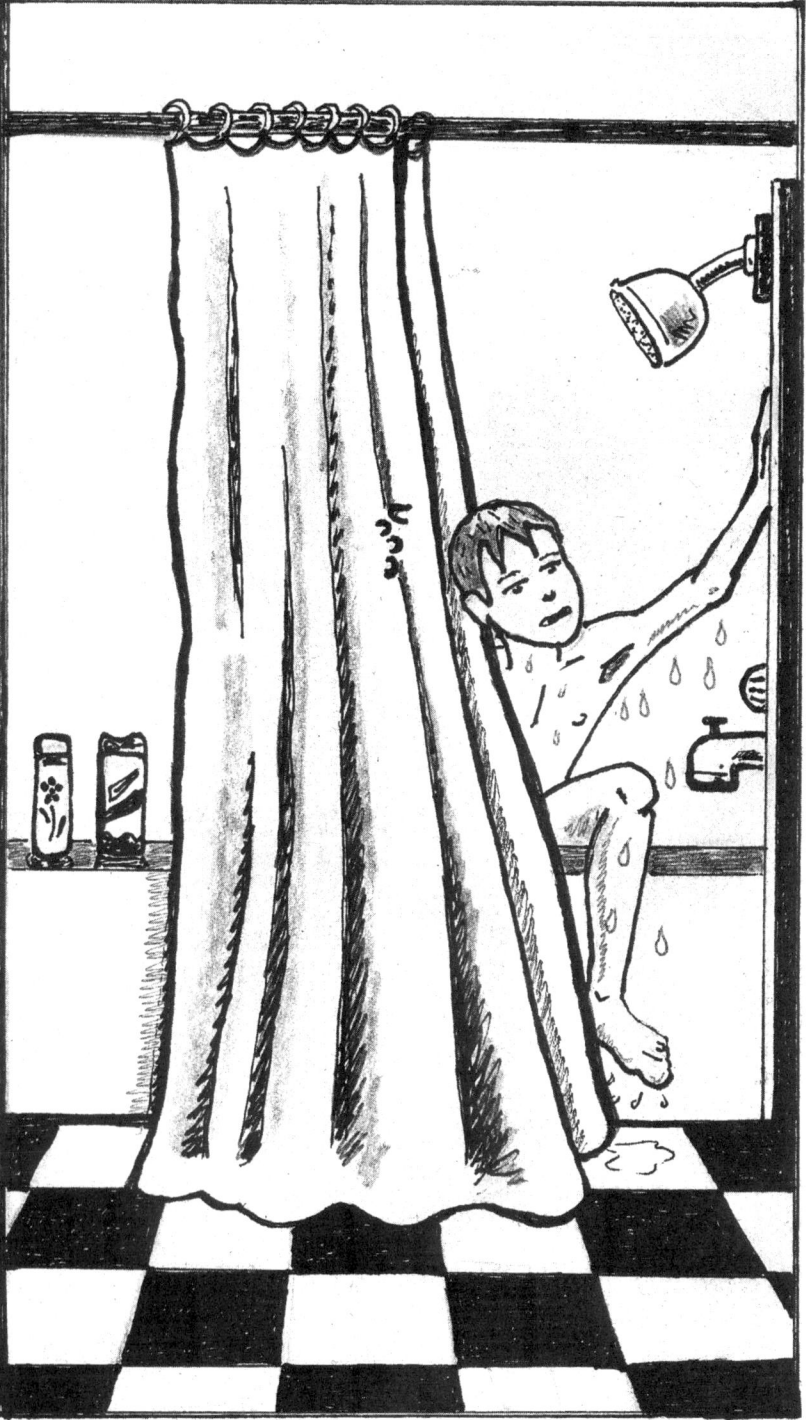

There was a big noise in the kitchen and then a yell! Willie slipped and lost his balance. With a big splash he fell out of the tub! He grabbed a towel and wrapped it around him. He ran into the kitchen to see what was the matter.

Ashley and Aunt Sandy stood there, covered from head to toe in flour. There was flour everywhere! They laughed so hard they could barely breathe.

"Willie," Aunt Sandy said, trying to catch her breath, "your sister just discovered the turbo high button on this new mixer of mine."

Ashley shook the flour from her hair. "Looks like I need to measure enough flour for another batch."

Aunt Sandy waved her hand in front of her and tried to clear the air. "This time let's make sure the flour goes into our pie instead of onto us!" She laughed again as she dusted off the girl's shoulders with a kitchen towel.

Willie enjoyed seeing his sister covered in flour. What he liked most was seeing the girl he thought was Little Miss Perfect actually making a mistake! But, of course, *she* didn't get in trouble for it. No one laughed at *his* homework mistake. He knew one thing for sure–no one would laugh at his *next* school project. He was really determined now.

But Willie still didn't have much to write about. *Okay, so I've seen–and smelled–some stinky pigs. And I've heard how people make peach pie from scratch. But is that all farming is about?* It was time to get dressed and get back to work.

Chapter 9

The Machine Shed

Willie walked into one of the three big metal buildings that were near the house. It was the biggest garage he had ever seen. There were all sorts of cool trucks and tractors everywhere.

"Are these your toys?" Willie asked.

"These are my tools, Willie," Uncle Kenny said. "When I plowed my first garden as a boy, I did things the old-fashioned way. We had two white mules named Jenny and Jake. I tied a hand plow to them—a plow loosens and turns the soil so you can plant. The mules would pull the plow as I walked behind, trying to keep it in a straight line. I had to work hard so my vegetables would grow in rows. I have a much bigger area to work now, so we use

51

tractors instead of mules. They don't get tired and they aren't as stubborn."

The farmer pointed to each piece of equipment in the shed and explained what it was. There were three tractors. Two of them looked really old. There was a tiller that loosened the dirt. The planter put the seeds in the ground.

Way back in the corner there was something covered up in a big white sheet. Willie figured there must be a secret hiding under it, because Uncle Kenny didn't talk about it. *Maybe it was a spaceship that crash-landed on his farm,* Willie thought. But the farmer acted as if it wasn't even there.

He pointed to the biggest machine Willie had ever seen. The tires were bigger than he was!

"This is my combine. It's what I use this time of year to harvest the crop. I can drive through the field and harvest six rows at a time. The combine

picks the corn, takes it off the cob, and even tells me how much per acre I collected."

"Let me guess what happens next," Willie said with a proud look. "You put the corn in cans and sell it to the grocery stores."

"Not quite, Willie. This is what's called *field corn*. After we finish our chores, it will be time to eat. We're having corn for supper. But it won't be coming out of a can."

Willie had a curious look on his face. *Are we going to eat just corn for supper?* he thought. *That's really bor---ing!*

Chapter 10

Something to Chew On

All of the chores were done. Willie was officially tired! He had just experienced his first full day on a farm—a very long day—and he had never worked so hard before. He was really hungry, but he wasn't excited about supper. That's because Uncle Kenny told him they were going to eat corn. He imagined a kitchen table piled high with ears of corn.

What are we going to have for dessert—popcorn? he wondered. *Supper is going to be super duper bor---ing.*

He looked around the entire kitchen. There was no corn anywhere.

"Uncle Kenny," Willie said, "I thought you said

we are having corn for supper."

"We are. There is corn all around you," he said as they sat down at the table.

The boy looked all around again. "I don't see any."

"A lot of the corn we grow is used to feed animals like pigs, cows, and chickens. So this pork roast is produced from corn. The gravy is made from cornstarch to make it thicker. That glass of milk is from dairy cows that eat corn. And tomorrow we'll have eggs for breakfast. The hens that lay the eggs feed on corn too."

Willie took a big bite of his salad. He was confused.

"By the way," Uncle Kenny pointed to the salad on the table, "your salad dressing is made from corn too."

"I see this salad dressing at the store." Willie looked closely at the ingredients on the bottle.

"Does that mean people everywhere eat things made out of corn?"

"You got it, Willie!" The farmer clapped his hands loudly. "People sitting down to eat in places like Arizona, New York, and Washington State are all eating corn in one way or another tonight for supper. And it doesn't stop there. A lot of our corn is put on ships and sent all around the world. Right now someone as far away as China is probably eating corn grown right here on our farm."

"That's awesome!" Willie shouted as he started to chow down on supper.

"And that's not all," Aunt Sandy added with a smile. "People all across this country are driving cars that run on ethanol fuel, which is made from corn."

"Wow! That's cool stuff!" Willie said. "But the people on the farm next to yours must not be very good farmers."

"Why is that, big fella?" the farmer asked with a curious look on his face.

"Because their corn is a lot shorter than yours."

The adults both laughed. "That isn't corn. Those are soybeans. We grow them too some years."

"What are they used for?" The boy reached for a homemade dinner roll.

"We are eating some soy too. And you see that candle?" Aunt Sandy said, pointing to the middle of the table. "It is made from soybeans. So is the ink used in our newspaper. And that is just the beginning. I printed some information for you from the farm bureau Web sites. I thought you might be interested."

Willie looked surprised. "You have the Internet here?"

"Sure!" she answered. "That's how we keep track of crop prices and download cheat sheets for video

games." The adults laughed. "Just kidding about that last part. Ashley was teaching me about that earlier."

"Well, I think that's enough learning for one day," Uncle Kenny said. "There is one more thing I think you should know about before you leave here, Willie. But for now, you better get some rest. Tomorrow comes earlier on the farm than in the city."

Willie wasn't quite sure what that meant, but he knew both his brain and his body were really tired. He wouldn't have any trouble getting to sleep tonight! He couldn't help but wonder what the farmer had planned for tomorrow.

Chapter 11

Neighbors

"Rise and shine!" A voice rattled Willie awake. There must be a mistake, Willie thought. *It's still dark outside.*

Willie got up and stretched big. He looked out the window and saw the sun just starting to come up over the hill. The sky was pink with light blue puffy clouds. He had never seen anything like it before. Maybe that was because he had never been up this early before!

He walked into the kitchen to find Uncle Kenny sipping on a huge mug of coffee. "I've already fed the animals. Gobble up your eggs, sleepyhead. We have some work to do!"

Willie shoveled in his breakfast and slipped on a

jacket. He walked out the door with a piece of toast in his mouth. He looked up to see the combine parked near the front porch.

"Jump in," the farmer said. "I have something I want you to be a part of."

Willie didn't even know how to get inside at first. Then he saw the steps that looked like a ladder and climbed in. From the front seat he felt like he was sitting on top of the world. He could see everything!

Uncle Kenny turned the key and started the combine. With a surge, the metal monster came to life.

"What are we going to do?" Willie asked.

Uncle Kenny checked all of the gauges. "We are going to find out what a neighbor is."

"That's easy. Everyone knows what a neighbor is," Willie said with a smirk. "It's someone who lives next door or down the street that my mom and dad

60

wave to as we drive by."

"Do you know their names?" the farmer asked.

"No, but we wave anyway."

As they talked, the combine drove away from Uncle Kenny's farm and onto the next farm. Uncle Kenny explained to Willie that a neighbor was injured on his tractor a couple of days ago. He had been driving along the gravel road on a tractor when a car came very close to him. That forced him to pull over too far. His tractor tipped over in the ditch and he fell under it. His left leg was broken.

"He has to stay in bed with his leg in a cast so that it can heal. That means he can't go out and harvest his crop. His wife, teenaged daughters, and young son are going to try to do it themselves this morning. But we have a surprise for them."

Uncle Kenny pulled up to the front of the home and stopped the combine. He and Willie walked to

the door and knocked.

"Good morning, Kenny," a woman said as she hugged the farmer. "And this must be Willie. Welcome to our farm." Although she smiled, her eyes looked red, like she'd been crying. "We were just finishing breakfast and sharing a prayer for the day. We're not quite sure how to get the crop in by ourselves, but we are determined to try. It's nice that you offered to come over and show us a few things to get us started."

Uncle Kenny reached for her hand and waved at her children to follow him. "I have something I want you to see." They walked to the back door. "Go ahead and open it."

She curiously opened the door, not sure what to expect. And there it was–the most awesome thing she had ever seen. Rows of combines and tractors lined up on their family farm, as far as they could

see. In front of the combines stood men and women from all over the area.

"Hope you don't mind," the farmer said. "We figured you might be able to use a hand or two to bring in that fine crop of yours. With all of us working together, we should get it done in no time."

The mother wiped away a tear with the back of her hand and smiled the biggest smile she could. She knew these farmers had plenty of their own work to do in their fields, but first they wanted to help their neighbor. Willie was happy to be one of the helpers. He had no idea he was about to become a real-life farmer!

Chapter 12

Farmer Willie

Willie had the time of his life watching all of the combines collect the corn.

"Do they get money for helping out?" Willie wondered out loud as he sat next to his uncle.

"No, the good feeling you get from helping others is payment enough, don't you think?" Uncle Kenny replied.

Willie remembered the good feeling he got when he brought his wagon full of pumpkins to the children in the hospital last year. "Yup. I sure do!"

The long day in the fields was coming to an end. Uncle Kenny lined up the combine to take in another six rows. He stopped and said, "Okay, big guy. It's your turn!"

"My turn for what?" Willie asked.

"Your turn to be a farmer." He smiled as he helped the boy get behind the steering wheel with him.

Together they put the big machine back to work, this time with Willie behind the wheel. He watched as the powerful combine chewed up row after row of corn. Pieces of yellow and brown stuff flew everywhere. Willie was harvesting his first crop!

"You think you have enough information to write your school paper?"

"I sure do! It's going to be the best report ever!" Willie looked at the corn and thought of his wagon. He had an idea. "I have to get home. I have a lot of work to do." He had big plans for himself–and for his wagon.

Chapter 13

Wagon Work

Willie was in his bedroom, finishing his report for school. He looked out the window and saw a lady with gray hair struggle with a heavy garbage bag. It was the same neighbor who waved to him as he left for the farm. She tried to get the big bag from the side of her house to the front curb.

"Excuse me!" Willie hollered out the window. "I will be right down to help you with that."

Willie ran down the stairs and into the garage. He opened the garage door and wheeled his wagon out. He pulled it down the sidewalk toward the home where he saw the woman. She waited to see what Willie was up to.

"Hi, my name is Willie," he said with a smile, holding out his hand for her to shake. "What is your name?"

"Hello, young man. I am Mrs. Wright," she answered.

"Could I help you with that bag? It would be a lot easier to move if we put it in my wagon."

"Thank you. That would be very nice," she said, admiring all of the colors on the wagon.

Together they pushed the heavy bag into the wagon. Willie rolled it to the curb.

The woman reached into her pocket and took out a couple of dollars. "Here is a little money for your work."

"No thanks, Mrs. Wright. I just wanted to be neighborly. Plus, that was kind of fun. I think I'll go down the street and see if anyone else needs some help."

"I'll go with you, if you like," she said. "I've lived here for a long time. I know most of the people who live on the street. I'll introduce you to them."

"Cool! Then I'll know all of my neighbors!"

Chapter 14

Back in Class

The school bell rang. All of the students quit talking and sat down at their desks.

"Before we get started, " Mrs. Specklefish began, "we had a nice long weekend–does anyone have anything to share with the class?"

Willie raised his hand.

"Willie, come on up."

Willie was nervous again. But this time it was the good kind of nervous. He was excited about what would happen next.

"I have this for you," he said as he handed his teacher a much longer report titled "What I Want to Be When I Grow Up."

"Is it okay if I share something else with the class?" Willie asked.

His teacher smiled and nodded.

Willie sped out of the room and into the hall. He looked back through the glass in the door. He could see the students lean forward and whisper to each other. He knew they had no idea what would come next. Most of them thought Willie was probably just going to get into trouble–again!

He looked at his mom, who waited for him in the hallway.

"Are you ready?" she asked.

"Yup. Let's go for it!"

She opened the classroom door for him. He asked the students to close their eyes and count from ten down to zero. They all started to count at once.

When they got to zero and opened their eyes,

Willie was standing at the front of the classroom. Beside him was his wagon.

"Cool," one student said.

"That wagon is awesome!" another yelled.

Willie reached into his wagon.

"What's inside? What's inside?" the students begged. One of them leaned so far over his desk to see that he almost tipped over.

Willie pulled out an ear of corn. He brought enough from the farm for every student to have one.

"I picked this for you. This is field corn, not sweet corn," he explained in a proud voice. "We eat it–but not in ways you think. Bet you didn't know that your favorite soda pop is made with corn syrup. The sweet flavor comes from cooking the kernels. Look what else I have in the wagon."

Willie held up a box of cereal, then a bag of chips and a box of cookies. "All of these are made

with corn. But we don't just eat the corn. Check this out!"

They got up from their desks and gathered around Willie and his wagon.

Willie reached into the wagon again. This time he held up a handful of soybeans. "These little guys are cool too. A lot of things we use in class are made from corn and soybeans. Some of your crayons, the chalk for the chalkboard, the tops of our desks, even the stuff that holds the carpet on the floor. And, oh yeah, the chewing gum we're not supposed to chew in class . . . you guessed it . . . it has corn and soybeans in it. And if you think that's cool? This is really cool. Who likes ice cream?"

"I do!" several students shouted, raising their hands.

"Ice cream can be made from both corn and soybeans!" Willie said proudly.

74

The students screamed and laughed and enjoyed this unique class project. Mrs. Specklefish watched and smiled. One of her uninspired students had now inspired the whole class to learn.

Willie was proud too. He couldn't wait to tell Uncle Kenny all about it.

Chapter 15

The Shed Surprise

That weekend Willie's parents drove him back to the farm. Before his uncle could even get off the porch to greet them, Willie burst out of the truck and ran toward him. He held his report up in the air.

Uncle Kenny looked at it and saw the big "E" on the top with a smiley face. "Does that mean ..."

"E is for excellent!" Willie interrupted with a yell. "We did it, we did it!"

Uncle Kenny looked over the rest of the report. He laughed when he read the last line out loud. "I want to be a farmer someday. Not because farming is easy, but because it's cool. Who else gets to say 'my job is feeding the world!' P.S. I almost forgot.

Farmers take care of the animals too. By the way, pigs will eat just about everything–including homework!"

They all laughed. Uncle Kenny bent down on one knee and said, "You worked very hard on this. I would like to share something special with you."

The farmer winked at Willie's parents and sister. They went into the house with Aunt Sandy, probably for more of that talking stuff.

Willie and his uncle walked into the machine shed. Willie remembered the first time he came in here. Uncle Kenny had showed him everything, except what was under that big white sheet. *Was it a spaceship?* he wondered. *Do I get to see it this time?*

Uncle Kenny walked right over to the mysterious covered object. He grabbed a corner and got ready to pull.

"We talked about how farmers work really hard,"

he said. "Well, sometimes we have fun on the farm too!"

He pulled off the cover. Underneath it was an old dune buggy car!

"Wow! That's cool!" Willie yelled with his eyes now wide open.

"My son bought this for me. He works for a company that tries to find new ways to make crops that feed more people. He thought we would enjoy fixing this buggy up together. Sometimes I use it to check on the crops. It's faster than my tractor and kind of fun to drive too. You worked hard on your school report. Let's say we have a little fun! Want to go for a ride?"

"You bet!" Willie answered, nearly jumping out of his shoes with excitement.

They drove along the hills and valleys with the wind blowing through their hair. Most of the corn

was already harvested. Uncle Kenny stopped before they got to the top of the biggest hill. Willie could see there was still some corn left in the field. "Willie, I am about to show you why I think this is the best job in the world."

He drove a little farther. And there it was. The sun was setting behind the last few rows of corn of the season. Their yellow stalks looked like gold, gently moving with the wind. The sunset painted the sky orange and purple with puffs of white and dark clouds.

"Woooow," Willie said in a quiet voice.

"You see, Willie, each spring we start with just the soil God gave us and a pair of healthy hands to work it. In the fall, we get to see what this beautiful land gives back. I've always believed that anything worth having is worth working for." He pointed at the crop. "So, what do you think?"

"I think I want to come back and see it in the springtime too. Can we stay here for a while?"

It was a strange feeling for Willie. There was nothing going on around him, but he wasn't bored.

They stood there silently and watched the sun set. It disappeared behind the last of the harvest. It was the coolest thing Willie had ever seen. And it was a moment in his life he knew he would never forget.

Gary Metivier has always considered himself a storyteller.

His love of writing probably started in the eighth grade. Instead of paying attention to his teacher, he was creating fictional characters that went on adventures. His stories pulled in his classmates, who would whisper for the "next page" as they secretly passed his work from desk to desk.

The shy boy–the tenth of twelve children–had found a creative outlet, and there was no looking back.

Not only did that same teacher, Janice Dillon Himegarner, inspire Gary to come out of his shell and reveal his character nearly 30 years ago, she helped copy-edit this book!

Gary still tells stories as an award-winning television news reporter, anchor, and now children's book writer. His first book, *Willie's Wagon*, became a bestseller within weeks of its release.

Gary lives in Davenport, Iowa, with his wife, Pam, and two young sons–Josh and Adam.

Illustrator David Houk has helped bring Willie to life in two books. David shares his passion for art with his elementary students in Davenport, Iowa. His mother, Stacey, is a big part of his inspiration. She is an art teacher too!

Go along with Willie on all of his adventures!

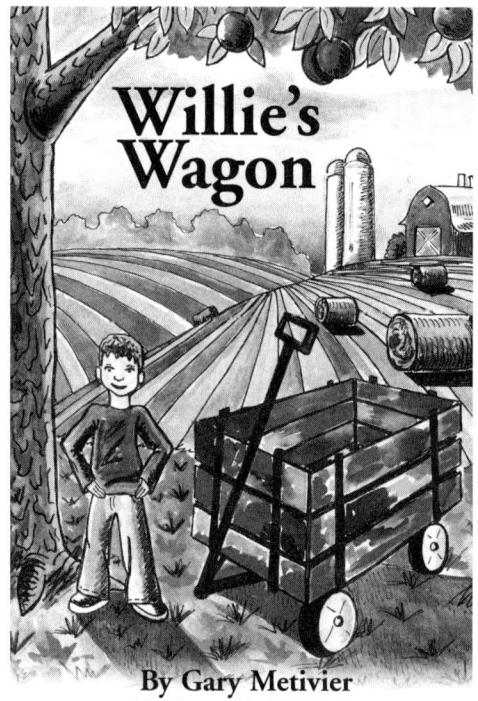

Willie's Wagon

By Gary Metivier
with a foreword by Bill Wundram

Visit
www.willieswagon.com
for more information